THE HEART OF THE WORLD

THE HEART OF THE WORLD

A SPIRITUAL CATECHISM

Thomas Keating

as told to
John Osborne

CROSSROAD · NEW YORK

1989
The Crossroad Publishing Company
370 Lexington Avenue, New York, NY 10017

Printed in the United States of America

Library of Congress Cataloging in Publication Data

Keating, Thomas.
The heart of the world.

Bibliography: p. 81
1. Spirituality.   2. Contemplation   I. Title.
BV4501.2.K37   248.3'4   81-684
ISBN 0-8245-0014-8   AACR2
ISBN 0-8245-0903-X (pbk)

Acknowledgments

All Biblical quotations are taken from THE REVISED STANDARD
VERSION OF THE BIBLE, Old Testament Section, Copyright 1952;
New Testament Section, First Edition, Copyright 1946; Second
Edition © 1971 by Division of Christian Education of the Na-
tional Council of the Churches of Christ in the United States of
America.

CONTENTS

PROLOGUE

As a member of a community of Cistercian monks since 1944, I have had the rare opportunity to absorb the contemplative tradition of Christianity within the context of monastic practice and experience. In recent years, my position in the community has brought me into contact with many Christians who remain almost totally unaware of the spiritual potential contained in their own tradition. They had turned to the East in the hope of finding a teaching and practice that would satisfy their hunger for spiritual experience. My own exposure to Eastern methods of meditation began in the 1960s. It awakened in me a deep appreciation of these values. These Eastern methods have expanded my understanding of the mystery of Christ and the message of the Gospel. Moreover, they mirror aspects of Christian mysticism overlooked in recent centuries. The contemplative dimension of life, present in all the great religions, is the common heart of the world. There the human family is already one.

"In our time," Pope John XXIII said on his deathbed, "we

1

should emphasize what unites rather than what divides." It is only with Vatican II that the Catholic Church explicitly embraced the values of the non-Christian religions and officially recognized in them the face of Christ; hidden no doubt, but truly present and revelaing the mystery of God.*

Although the recognition of the values of the non-Christian religions is a step forward, it is only the beginning. It is a fact that the message of Christ has never really been preached in a non-Western frame of reference. We inherited the Greco-Roman world view, and it was through the Fathers of the early Church, most of whom were Neoplatonists, that the mystery of Christ was originally explained in theological terms. It was explained in the Middle Ages by St. Thomas Aquinas and others in terms of Aristotelian philosophy. More recently, efforts have been made to express Christianity in terms of phenomenology, existential philosophy, and Marxism. But up until very recently it has not been presented in terms that would be understandable to Eastern culture and tradition.

The genuine traditions of spirituality of the East and Christianity are coming together in a confrontation that should be complementary rather than contradictory. Christianity and the great religions of the East have developed distinctive approaches to the Absolute which could significantly enrich each other. The aspects of Eastern spirituality which could be of special value to Christianity today are: the importance of contemplation as the source of action, the illusory nature of our subjective view of the world, the experience of non-duality, and the practice of techniques which help to integrate the mind and body.

We will be in a better position both to examine the religious experience of the East and to represent our own tradition if we

*Declaration on the Relationship of the Church to NonChristian Religions, in *The Documents of Vatican II*, ed. Walter Abbott (New York: Herder and Herder, 1966), p. 660.

can first rediscover the forgotten richness of contemplative Christianity. The transcendent as well as the immanent dimensions of Christ must be recovered from ancient and medieval Christian tradition.

This book emerges from the conviction that the tradition of Christian spirituality and mystical wisdom needs to be presented today as an integral part of the proclamation of the Gospel and of Christian education. It is news to most of our contemporaries that there is such a thing as a Christian spirituality which can be experienced.

This book is an attempt to outline the principles of that spirituality for those in the Christian community who are eager to incorporate a contemplative dimension into their lives. This book is also for Christians who have turned East for spiritual experience and who now would like to integrate that experience into their Christian background. Finally, it is addressed to those of other spiritual traditions who are interested in dialogue with the Christian tradition.

The original inspiration for this book came from John Osborne in the fall of 1977. As a student at Yale Divinity School and of Eastern methods of meditation, he visited me in the hope of discovering ways of integrating his studies and meditation practice into his Christian training and background. He was representative of many others I had already met who were students of Zen, Insight Meditation, Transcendental Meditation, and other Eastern practices. My interest in John's concerns prompted him to make a tape recording of two of our conversations. Later he circulated these among friends and colleagues who were also looking for an expression of their Christian faith in terms of spirituality and experience. Their favorable reaction, along with encouragement from other sources, prompted me to think that this material might be useful as an introduction to contemplative Christianity. With John's assistance, I edited the original taped conversations and expanded them from their question and answer format to the present form of this book. John and I want to thank the many people at St. Joseph's Abbey and elsewhere who helped with criticism and encouragement over the past three years. Helen Gallahue and Carl Gossman managed the difficult task of typing revisions.

Thomas Keating

1

THE MESSAGE OF MONASTIC LIFE

It might be easiest to begin with an introduction to the particular kind of Christian life which has been the guardian of so much of Christian spirituality throughout the ages. Christian monasticism dates from the early part of the fourth century. It sprang up almost simultaneously in Egypt, Syria, and Asia Minor. While it expressed its inspiration in various concrete forms, all of them shared the same fundamental dedication to the search for God through silence, solitude, simplicity of lifestyle, and spiritual development. These spiritual values were generally lived within a community which provided an environment conducive to the search for God.

Spiritual development is the birthright of every man and woman, not only of cloistered monks and nuns. Monastic life is simply a professional way of going about it. While the world as a whole tends to neglect and forget the knowledge of how to pursue and live a spiritual life, the monastic world has been occupied through the ages in trying to preserve that knowledge. At this moment of history, there are large numbers of genuine seekers after truth. Many of them never had a specific commitment to one of the Christian denominations, or even to any religion. Others, who were raised as Christians or Jews, never heard any challenge to lead an interior life of prayer and union with God in their local churches or church-related schools.

During the last three or four centuries, the Christian spirituality of earlier times has become lost to view, and it is principally in monasteries that a continuing tradition of contemplation has been handed down. For this reason many of these seekers, both Christian and non-Christian, are turning to monasteries for some kind of guidance. This is especially true since the Vatican Council (1961–1965), which set in motion a vast program for the spiritual renewal of the Roman Catholic Church. This movement has awakened the interest of those in other Christian churches and in other religions who are seeking the spiritual renewal of their own traditions.

A contemplative monastery is a visible sign of our common human groping for interiority or wholeness and for what is deepest in human values. It is the sign of the Church's groping for the fulness of the Christian mystery — oneness with God and with all creation. The monastic life-style is designed to lead those who enter it into a new attitude towards all reality. A certain measure of solitude and silence, and the practice of the traditional vows of poverty, chastity, and obedience, reduce the distracting stimuli which reinforce our view of ourselves and the world. This gradual silencing of our habitual ways of thinking and reacting opens up our awareness to other realities and other values, especially the value of every other human being at the deepest level. The ultimate purpose of monastic life is to experience oneness with everyone else — and to bear all the consequences of that experience.

A certain experience of God is quite common in the population. People do not talk about it because they think that if they mention their experience to their friends, everyone will think they are crazy. People who are not even religiously minded have an experience of transcendence now and then, but they do not know how to articulate it. If they should hear a few words indicating knowledge of an experience which is beyond thoughts, which is very peaceful, and which arises spontaneously, this will awaken memories of experiences which were very real to them at one time. We have to begin to understand that it is *normal* to be contemplative; it just needs to be cultivated.

Have you ever experienced a few moments of interior silence? How would you describe it? Is there not a sense of a very deep, all-pervading peace, a sense of well-being, and a delicate joy, all at once? Why is it such a difficult state to maintain or return to? It seems easier to forget about the whole experience than to be plagued by the pain of lingering outside a door that seems to be locked from the inside. Yet, in spite of this lingering pain, the repeated experience of interior silence is a need that everyone has in order to be fully human. Our capacity for the transcendent is precisely what distinguishes us most from the rest of visible creation. It is what makes us most human.

Not long ago a group of university students visited the Abbey on a field trip in connection with a course in mysticism they were taking in school. After a few brief introductions, they wanted to know about my past life, my reasons for entering the monastery, and what possessed me to reach such a decision. Having answered as best I could without completely undermining my reputation, I said to them, "May I now ask you a question? Have you ever experienced a few moments of interior silence?"

They thought about that for a few moments, and then, very gradually, began to respond. I doubt if any of them were church-goers. Their professor said later that their interest in Christian mysticism did not coincide with church-going, at least not much of it. It was intriguing to hear four or five of these young people discuss their various experiences of interior silence.

So I pursued it a little further. "What was it like?"

One girl said, "I can remember a few times when I was lying on my bed, and a sense of well-being came over me along with deep interior silence, peace and joy. The only trouble with it was that I couldn't make it last. There was also no way of getting back to it after it had gone."

Another made this observation: "It is like having a door inside of you that is normally closed. You would like to get in, but can't; and yet, every now and then, it just opens up. The feeling is just wonderful. It is like coming home."

I said, "Well, you can't make it come about then?"

Several replied at once, "No."

I said, "If you can't bring it about, who is it that opens the door?"

They were not prepared to answer that question, except that they knew it was not themselves. As a result of experiencing these moments of interior silence, they seem never to have forgotten the occasions, even if they happened only once. Evidently, the experiences had made a great impression and had influenced their actions for some time afterward. But little by little they faded away, as the students got immersed once again in the daily round. One other point made by these young people was that the experience of inner silence was like being really one's true self for a few moments, rooted in one's self. It was a deep affirmation of their being.

From this encounter we learn that interior silence is a fairly frequent and even ordinary human experience. It is not something given only to very spiritual or holy people. It seems to respond to a real need, as real and vital as eating or sleeping. You can survive, of course, without moments of interior silence, while you cannot survive without eating or sleeping; but a question could be raised about the quality of your survival. If this spiritual need is not appeased, it will take revenge in strange ways, such as an uncomfortable hunger. We may find ourselves trying to cover up the remembrance of this hunger in order not to feel its pangs. A lot of compulsive behavior — drugs, sexual license, hyper-activity, work for work's sake — can be means of escaping from the awareness of this hunger. Nature seems to have provided us with the need of interior silence. We seek it as we seek returning to a place of security, warmth, and love. Christian revelation addresses itself to this natural tendency and tells us *who* it is that opens the door and lets us in.

A contemplative monastery is a visible expression of the fact that a state or place of interior silence is really available to all, and that everyone is invited. Such a place possesses a mysterious fascination. People do not come merely to look at the liturgy. They do not come just to sniff incense or pick up religious vibrations in the church. They feel intuitively that a contemplative monastery has something they are looking for. The buildings suggest it; the solitude suggests it; the silence suggests it. A group of people seeking interior silence as a life's work is a call to others to do something similar in their lives. This call is a significant service in our day; one, however, that is impossible to measure with any kind of tool.

But what are the consequences of responding to this call?

When you reduce the ordinary flow of thoughts and your emotional reactions to them, you enter into a new world of reality. Even on the level of the senses we hear sounds only within a certain frequency or see things at a certain distance. Dogs hear much more than we do. Hawks see much farther than we do. If the range of our senses is limited in these areas, it should be no surprise that there are other levels of awareness that our ordinary sense experiences do not perceive either. This is especially true of the level of spiritual reality, which is the level of the mysteries of the Christian faith. Ordinary hearing does not grasp them. Ordinary seeing does not perceive them. Thus, Jesus repeatedly reminded his listeners, "He that has ears to hear, let him hear" (Matt. 11:15), hinting that we must develop a greater capacity for hearing than the external ear alone. Christian tradition teaches that there are faculties of finer spiritual perception which develop in a climate of interior silence.

The principal means monks use to cultivate interior silence—external silence, a certain measure of solitude, and a non-possessive attitude—can be put into a concentrated form, like a *capsule*, to be taken daily, or several times a day. The traditional word for this is contemplative prayer.

Mary of Bethany gives us an example of how we might proceed. In the Gospel of Luke we read that "she seated herself at the Lord's feet and listened to His teaching" (Luke 10:39). It is clear from the remarks of Jesus in her defense that she was engaged in some special kind of activity of greater value than Martha's in preparation of his meal. Mary was listening to the Word of God—the divine person—a reality deeper than the human words falling upon her sense of hearing and resounding in her imagination. She was listening with her whole being. Her identity was melting into the presence of the Word of God within her. John, resting in the bosom of Jesus at the Last Supper, prayed in the same way that Mary of Bethany listened. He was not thinking or talking, but *resting*.

Contemplative prayer allows the hunger and thirst for God to well up. "On the last and great day of the Feast, Jesus stood up in the Temple and cried out with a loud voice: 'If any man thirst, let him come to me and drink. Out of his inmost being will flow rivers of living water. This he said of the Holy Spirit who was to be given to those who believe'" (John 7:37–38). By these words, we are urgently invited to put aside our preoccupations and come to Christ in the depth of our being. This movement and the experience which results from it are the basis for every genuine form of Christian spirituality.

2

CHRISTIAN SPIRITUALITY

For the early Fathers of the Church there was only one spirituality, the spirituality of Jesus Christ, who died and rose again, and who is pouring out his Spirit over the world. As time went on, the richness of the mystery of Christ tended to be differentiated. Christ is too big a reality to be fully expressed by any one individual or any one vocation. Yet all expressions, all vocations, must be rooted in him.

The apostolic expression was powerful in the early Church and is especially strong again today as it works for world peace, justice, and service of the poor. On the other hand, there are always persons who are called by the Spirit to a greater participation in the mystery of Christ's silence and solitude through a life organized for the growth of contemplation. There is no opposition between action and contemplation. Rather, it is a question of emphasis and of one's aptitude and vocation from God. The institutional life-styles that gradually evolved over the centuries have become known as the active and contemplative lives.

But there are further differentiations. Various religious move-

11

ments have been raised up by the Spirit in the course of the centuries to meet certain needs of the time. Each movement has a special spirituality that goes back to the particular vision of its founder. But these particularities must not be emphasized to the detriment of the ultimate spirituality which belongs to every Christian. This ultimate reality is the indwelling Spirit who makes of us a temple of God, Father, Son and Holy Spirit. This one point needs to be strongly emphasized: every Christian, by virtue of the grace of baptism, *has* the vocation to oneness with the Father through Jesus Christ in the Holy Spirit.

Everyone needs some kind of practice in order to accomplish this vocation. Obviously, a rule of life cannot be as detailed for those living in the world as it is for people in a monastery. But everyone has to build his or her own kind of enclosure as far as one's duties allow, by setting aside a certain amount of time every day for prayer and spiritual reading. Also, perhaps, one may dedicate a day every month, and a week every year, to being alone with the Lord. Jesus himself encouraged this in the Gospel when he said to the apostles, "Come away by yourselves to a lonely place, and rest a while" (Mark 6:31).

It is difficult to establish a rule of life to which one is faithful without the help of other similarly minded persons. A spiritual friend or a prayer group sharing similar values can be a great help in maintaining one's enthusiasm for growth in union with Christ. This help can be mutually sustaining during the inevitable slacking-off periods that occur because of circumstances or human weakness. All these particular recommendations could be summed up by saying that a contemplative understanding of Christ's teaching has to be firmly grounded in *experience.* There are two kinds of spiritual experience which might cause confusion unless we distinguish them carefully: one is interior, the other active. The spiritual experience that comes through the development of interior prayer is the result of the influx of divine love and the contemplative gifts of the Holy Spirit. Divine love illumines the mysteries of faith and enables one to begin to taste the sweetness and goodness of God through the gift of wisdom. This awakens enthusiasm in the whole of one's being.

The second kind of spiritual experience translates that enthusiasm into concrete action. This is what is meant by the practice of virtue. We do not practice virtue for its own sake, although it is helpful in learning to calm our emotions and to dispose us for contemplation. We practice virtue out of love for Christ. One of the best ways to do this is to seek God's will as it manifests itself in ordinary circumstances and events. This seeking to please God and to give up the obstacles in us which prevent us from doing his will with alacrity are essential to Christian practice. Without this effort in our daily lives, one can doubt the genuine character of the interior experiences, however glamorous or inspiring. Interior experience is geared to action. It is designed to soften up our self-centered dispositions, to deliver us from what is compulsive in our motivation, and to open us up completely to God and to the genuine service of others.

The criterion of true Christian spirituality, affirmed by the Gospel over and over again, is the practical and concrete love of neighbor which leads us to make the sacrifice of our own desires, convenience, and comfort, in order to meet the needs of others. Christ's commandment goes even further: "Love one another *as I have loved you*" (John 15:12). What is this essential aspect of Christ's love, and how can we live it?

The love of Christ manifested itself in his sheer vulnerability. The crucifix is the sign and expression of the total vulnerability of Jesus: the outstretched arms, the open heart, the forgiveness of everything and everyone. This sheer vulnerability made him wide open both to suffering *and* to joy.

It was this vulnerability that caused him to experience the pain of Judas' betrayal, as well as the joy of celebrating the Pasch with his disciples.

If there had been no possibility of betrayal, there could have been no Eucharist. If the disciples were to be admitted to his intimate friendship, there could only be loneliness and disappointment when they all abandoned him and fled. Only in the heart of one with boundless readiness to forgive could there have been the pain of Peter's triple denial, and afterwards the joy of reinstating him as chief of the apostles.

If Jesus were to hear a word of repentance from the good thief, he had to listen to the mockery of the bad thief.

If Jesus were to receive the consoling sympathy of the women of Jerusalem, he had to endure the hatred and contempt of those who took pleasure in his death.

If it had not been possible for him to experience abandonment by the Father, there could not have been an infinite depth to his total gift of himself to the Father.

If there had not been a soldier to open his side with the lance, there could have been no water and blood, symbols of the life-giving sacraments, flowing from his side.

If Jesus had not actually died on the Cross, the holy women could not have anointed his body for burial.

If he had not been buried in the tomb, he could not have risen from the dead.

Vulnerability means to be hurt over and over again without seeking to love less, but more. Divine love is sheer vulnerability — sheer openness to giving. Hence, when it enters the world, either in the person of Jesus or in one of his disciples, it is certain to encounter persecution — death many times over. But it will also encounter the joy of ever rising again. "For love is stronger than death... Many waters cannot quench it" (Song of Sol. 8:6-7). Being vulnerable means loving one another as Christ loved us. If we did not have to forgive people, we would have no way of manifesting God's forgiveness toward us. People who injure us are doing us a great favor because they are providing us with the opportunity of passing on the mercy that we have received. By showing mercy, we increase the mercy we receive. The best way to receive divine love is to give it away, and the more we pass on, the more we increase our capacity to receive.

Scripture speaks of the human race as "all flesh" (Gen. 9:11) to emphasize its corporate identity. Paul taught that the whole human family suffered because of the action of one man and was redeemed through the action of one man, namely, Jesus Christ (Rom. 5:12-19). While this intuition into the oneness of the human family is extremely important, we must also emphasize the fact that we are saved not only as a vast multitude, but individually, one by one. There needs to be a balance between these two insights. There is a personal and a social dimension to every human being. We need to be conscious of our responsibility to both.

Paul, in developing the idea of the human body as an image of the Mystical Body of Christ, wrote, "If one member suffers, all suffer together" (1 Cor. 12:26). The organic oneness of the human family achieved still greater unity by being incorporated into God's Son through his incarnation and resurrection. This oneness of the human family is an aspect of the mystery of Christ that needs strong emphasis today. It cuts across the differences of race, creed, color, or nationality. It requires us to respect religious and cultural differences rather than oppose them. Moreover, these differences are often complementary when properly understood, and point to the cosmic Christ. The gospel parable of the Good Samaritan means that our neighbor is anyone at all—anywhere—who is in need. In the Old Testament we are told, "When you see the naked, to cover him, and not to hide yourself from your own flesh" (Isa. 58:7). In other words, anyone who is suffering is one of us. We should feel the weight of his or her need because it is also our own.

3

SACRIFICE

The best way to begin to experience the transcendent dimension of Christ is by studying his life and teaching as recorded in the Gospels. The scriptures, especially Christ's own words, are written out of a very deep level of consciousness. They are efficacious on whatever level they are received, but obviously our penetration of the meaning of the words will depend on our present level of consciousness. That is why the same text of scripture keeps striking the eager reader as constantly new. It is always opening up new levels of meaning, not because the words are changing, but because *we* are changing as our faith deepens and we are better prepared to listen.

In the Gospel Jesus kept urging his listeners to be alert: "He who has ears to hear, let him hear" (Matt. 11:15). This is an invitation to deepen our capacity to hear him. As our capacity for listening grows, so does our understanding of his message. Our relationship to Christ, to our neighbor, and to ourselves all begin to take on a different perspective. Every new level of faith transforms our world, because it gives us a whole new view of

17

reality. As our level of consciousness becomes more spiritual, the whole of creation takes on new meaning. It is no longer so opaque, so contradictory; no longer a world of opposites. Because of our new perspective, we perceive that many seeming contradictions are really complementary at a higher level of consciousness. As we move up the ladder of faith, our philosophical questions tend to recede. As trust in God becomes greater, fewer questions arise.

The love which the Father has for Christ is offered to each of us all the time. It does not bring the perfect fulfillment which is to be found in heaven, but it is an anticipation of that joy. "Come to me, all you who labor and are heavy laden," Jesus said, "and I will give you rest" (Matt. 11:28). The word "rest" has a precise tradition in Christian spirituality. The early contemplative monks of the Egyptian deserts understood this term to mean something much more than sitting under a heavenly palm tree. Rather, they were thinking of the "rest" that comes from wanting what God wants and not being compulsively forced to do their own will, because their own will, along with everything else in their ego, had been sacrificed to God. Sacrifice is absolutely essential for human growth; yet the abiding disposition of sacrifice is rarely established without some experience of suffering. Of course suffering itself does not make one holy and can even lead to despair. Despair is suffering that fails to teach.

A clear distinction must be made between sacrifice and suffering. Suffering is the conscious experience of pain. Sacrifice can also involve conscious pain, but it is primarily an attitude. The attitude of sacrifice can transform suffering into joy. We bring many needless sufferings on ourselves, and these God does not will. But to suffer as a member of a fallen race and to endure the consequences of the human condition is what the Son of God himself did. This form of suffering may be an important part of our purification. God may also send suffering to people who are already thoroughly purified as a counterweight to the effects of moral evil in the world. This is called vicarious suffering. Most of the great religions of the world recognize this mystery.

The mystery of vicarious suffering is most clearly revealed in the crucifixion of Jesus Christ. There innocence itself was destroyed in order to redeem the human family. If God's only-begotten Son can suffer and die, the suffering and death of the innocent take on a wholly new dimension. It likewise can be seen as redemptive. Faith alone can perceive God triumphing in the midst of human suffering and bringing about the reign of divine love.

"God is love" (1 John 4:16). When divine love overflows from the interior life of the Trinity into our hearts, it immediately confronts our false selves, and we experience conflict. A struggle arises between this pure goodness — sheer giving — and the ingrained possessiveness, aggressiveness, and self-seeking which are so characteristic of us in our present condition. Thus, at the very heart of life is the challenge of sacrifice; of dying to our present condition in order to move to a higher level of life. This can only happen by letting go of the false self.

Suffering and death are not enemies, but doors leading to new levels of knowledge and of love. Unless we are willing to sacrifice what we have now, we cannot grow. We grow by dying and rising again; by dying to where we are now and being reborn at a new level.

Paul tells us to look to Christ "who for the joy set before him endured the cross, despising the shame" (Heb. 12:2). This is an important insight in trying to understand suffering. What is normally experienced as painful at one level of our evolving consciousness is not necessarily experienced as painful when we move to a higher level on the ladder of consciousness. It is obvious among the saints of all religions that, although they led incredibly difficult and arduous lives, they experienced joy in those very hardships. Hardship itself seems to have become joy. The same kind of life would have meant intolerable suffering for the average person.

Thus, we have to understand first of all what is meant by *suffering*, and then relate it to the person who is undergoing it before making a judgment. It is misleading to think that all aches and pains are going to disappear as one climbs the ladder of consciousness. On the other hand, one's attitude toward suffering is going to change. It may change to such a degree that the experience itself becomes a joy; not for its own sake, but because it is perceived to be a participation in the mystery of Christ's passion — a way of sacrificing oneself in order to express, to the utmost degree, one's dedication to God. As one comes to know God more intimately, the heart expands, and the desire for union with him tends to put all obstacles and hardships into the shade; to make them seem, while nonetheless real, not worth thinking about.

Through the revelation of the Trinity, we have come to realize that the inner nature of infinite being is the mystery of a love that is totally self-giving. The English word "love" does not bring out the nuances of the Greek term used in the New Testament texts, which is usually translated "charity" and which means a totally self-giving love — a love that is self-*less*.

Divine love is not a feeling of benevolence. It is not a feeling at all. It is *total* self-giving. There is no self-interest in the Trinity. Each person of the Trinity dwells in the others, and everything that they have is shared in common. The only distinction is the *way* in which each shares the infinite treasure of the Godhead. The Father shares it to give it, the Son to receive it, and the Holy Spirit to rejoice in it as the gift of the Father and the Son. When divine love invades the world of broken people, a world in which there is suffering and limitation, it is certain to be rejected. It is precisely by being rejected, and yet still remaining steadfast in boundless compassion, that its divine character is ultimately proved. Moreover, divine love triumphs over every obstacle, including suffering and death. This is why the passion of Jesus is the most magnificent and comprehensive revelation of divine love that exists. It reveals the ultimate meaning of reality, which is sacrifice. In a world of imperfection, divine love is proved by sacrifice.

Jesus faced a great dilemma in sacrificing himself for the redemption of the human family. As Son of God, he was one with the Father and knew the beauty and goodness of God and the ugliness and hatefulness of sin as no other human being could ever perceive them. Yet, in the Garden of Gethsemane he was called upon by his Father, as Paul says, "to *be* sin" (2 Cor. 5:21); that is, to take upon himself the actual experience of the sinner, with the sinner's feelings of guilt and self-rejection, and, what is worst of all, his sense of alienation from God.

This was the incredible double-bind that Jesus had to struggle with in his agony in the Garden of Gethsemane: "Father, how can *I*, your *Son*, become *sin*?" In Jesus, at that moment, the ultimate opposites met. No opposites could ever be further apart than these. He knew it was the Father's will that he accept the terrible anguish of the experience of alienation from Him. For Jesus, this was excruciating in the extreme, for he knew the Father as no one else could ever know him. His response was total self-surrender to the Father: "Not my will, but *thine* be done" (Luke 22:42). But it caused him to sweat blood.

The attainment to the heights of the spiritual life does not take away all suffering. It *may*, but it may *not*. Christ did not suffer because of the kind of upside-down human nature with which most of us have to struggle. He was suffering because it was the will of the Father that he take upon himself the sins of the world in order to free us from their consequences. It was by identifying himself with our state of sinfulness with all its consequences that he utterly destroyed it. Thus, at the moment of death he triumphed over sin. At that moment, as John says so significantly, "He handed over the spirit" (John 19:30).

The Spirit was received by the disciples as tongues of fire on the day of Pentecost. The new power which overwhelmed them was based on an invincible confidence in Jesus, emerging from their newly awakened awareness of sonship and intimacy with the Father. Salvation is fundamentally the realization of oneness with God. When we work to surrender our own desires, world view, self-image, and all that goes to make up the false self, we are truly participating in Christ's emptying of himself, as Paul described it. We are emptying ourselves of the false self so that our true self, which is the Christ-life in us, may express itself in and through our human faculties. And we can do this because he handed over his human life to the Father, and at the same time he handed over the Divine Spirit to the human family.

Jesus said, "If anyone would come after me, let him deny himself and take up his cross and follow me" (Matt. 16:24). What is this "self"? It is our thoughts, feelings, self-image, and world view. Jesus added, "Whoever would save his life will lose it, and whoever loses his life for my sake, will find it" (Matt. 16:25). That is, he will find eternal life, the Christ-life, welling up within.

Faith is not just the acceptance of abstract propositions about God; it is the total surrender of ourselves to God. In baptism, our false self is put to death and the victory won by Christ is placed at our disposal. The dynamic set off in baptism is meant to increase continuously during the course of our chronological lives and lead to the experience of the risen life of Christ within us. In the Christian view, death is thus an integral part of living. Dying to the false self is the movement from a lower form of life to a higher one; from a lower state of consciousness to a higher state of consciousness; from a weak faith to a faith that is strong, penetrating, and unifying.

Participation in the life of Christ means coming to know and love the person of Jesus. The humanity of Christ is our starting point and the door into his divinity. Jesus said, "I am the door of the sheepfold. If anyone enters by me, he shall go in and out and find pasture" (John 10:7-9). We enter through the knowledge and love of Christ's humanity into the sheepfold of his divinity, where he invites us to rest in oneness of spirit. The new person that comes to birth in that deep interior rest manifests Christ in the place and time in which he or she lives.

4

THE INCARNATION

According to the Gospel of John, Jesus Christ is the personal expression of the Father. The Father in Christian tradition is the uncreated source of the divine nature, the silence of the Godhead from which the eternal Word emerges. "At the beginning God expressed himself," John says. "This personal expression, this *Word*, was with God and was God" (John 1:1). This interior Word, this self-awareness arising continually from the Father's infinite silence, remains interiorly united to him (John 1:18). When these two infinite persons confront each other in the fulness of their intimate knowledge of each other, there flows eternally from their common heart a breath of love, a sigh of infinite satisfaction and bliss, which we call the Holy Spirit.

The Word took flesh of the Virgin Mary and became the historical man, Jesus. Although this divine person became man at an historical moment, he remained always present to every human being — past, present, and to come — in his divine person. As man, he is the anointed one foretold by the prophets of the Old Testament — anointed not only with a special grace, but with the fulness of the Godhead — *possessed* by the divine person of the Word of God. Christ's human nature is God's way of showing us how to be human in the complete sense of the term. Just as the Word is the full expression of the Father, so Jesus is the fullest human revelation of God that can be given to us.

A saint or prophet, however holy or great, always retains his own distinct personality and individuality as possessor of his own particular human nature. Indeed, it is the complete submission of his human nature and personality to the Spirit of God that makes him a kind of incarnation of God; but an incarnation of God only in an analogous sense — in a partial, limited sense. However, a Christian believes that the man Jesus is united to the person of the Word without limitation or mediation. What is involved is not the union of two persons, but the unity of a single person.

Since the person possessing the human nature of Jesus is the eternal Son of God, Jesus is not confined to the period of history in which he lived his human life. The life of Jesus is not just for his own time and for the time that has come after him, but is for men and women of *all* time. His redeeming work has been available to every member of the human family from the beginning of the world. This perspective involves what might be called *vertical time*: the eternal values breaking into horizontal or chronological time. The latter is the time that we experience as our historical lifetime. Thus, at each moment of our lives the eternal values that have come into the world through Christ are available to everyone as historical time unfolds. Our historical lifetime is given us precisely to grow into vertical time, which scripture calls "eternal life." It is this meeting of the horizontal and vertical dimensions of time in Christ that gives the cross its tremendous power as a symbol of all reality.

In the spiritual disciplines of the great religions of the East, the emphasis is on emptying the mind of concepts. To those who follow these traditions, therefore, the idea of going to the Absolute through a *man* seems like a second-rate procedure. Anyone who has experienced transcendence is likely to reject that procedure. Even though no one claims complete control of transcendent experiences, especially those that are sublime, a person who is exposed to such experiences is aware that this kind of knowledge vastly surpasses anything that can come from the imagination or the reflections of the intellect. Moreover, the experience of transcendence is extremely reassuring. It is like coming home. There is a mysterious peace and security that come from approaching — and seeming to touch — the spiritual level of our nature. Since we are spiritual as well as corporeal beings, our nature is fundamentally capable of spiritual experience and enjoys having it.

God has made all kinds of creatures. A flower turns its face to the sun, and if it could speak, would say, "Here I am." Just being a flower is the glory that it gives to God. But a human being is made differently; we are not just material creatures. What distinguishes us from the rest of material creation is freedom. It is when, with our capacity for acting freely, we turn to God and say, "Here I am," that we begin to glorify our Creator.

At the same time, it is not enough to have transcendent experiences. We have to translate those experiences into daily life and into our humdrum routine. We have to bring all our faculties into harmony with higher states of consciousness and express that knowledge in human terms, in the dusts of this world.

When people who lived with Jesus looked at him, he seemed to be like any other ordinary man from life's highway. The Jewish people of that period were expecting a Messiah in a heroic mold, a political hero who would work fantastic miracles to establish his own particular power structure. Instead, Jesus identified with the powerless and with the materially poor, rather than with the rich and powerful of his time. This is what got him into trouble.

Jesus really is a man. He is fully human, body, soul and spirit. And yet we believe, as Christians, that this is the Son of God. Without confusion of his divine and human natures, he is the absolute in human form. Perhaps we can understand Jesus' identity as the Son of God more clearly by thinking of him in terms of the revelation of the Trinity. That revelation affirms what the mystics of all religions have intuited: that the ultimate nature of infinite being is love. God, the ultimate reality, the absolute, in a way beyond our comprehension, is a community of persons. As the Father has life in himself and pours it into his Son, and they rejoice in it together in the procession of the Holy Spirit, so the Son who has life in himself, shares the divine life with the whole human family through the outpouring of the Holy Spirit, and invites everyone to the banquet of eternal life. The revelation of the Trinity, the greatest mystery of the Christian religion, is the essential model, not only for understanding, but for living and experiencing the Christian life.

"He who has seen me," Jesus said, "has seen the Father" (John 14:9). The Word of God was always present beyond time. In the incarnation, he became present *in* time. He enfolds us, therefore, both within the temporal sphere and beyond it, at one and the same time. As the bride in the Song of Solomon said, "His left hand is under my head and his right hand ready to embrace me" (Song of Sol. 2:6). His left hand signifies the dimension of time and his right hand the dimension of eternity. With the two arms of his human and divine natures, he enfolds us in the mystery of the incarnation in an incredibly strong embrace.

There are those who know Christ beyond time as "the true light that enlightens everyone" (John 1:9). We must bring them the good news of Christ *inside* of time, so that all true seekers of God may experience his full embrace. However, we Christians must not cling too closely to the Christ *inside* of time. Rather, we must allow him to bring us to the knowledge of himself *beyond* time. We must know Jesus, not only in his beginning, but in his end, not only in the crib, but in his ascension. For we too have come from the bosom of the Father and must find our home there. Christ in his divine being is present in your heart, in mine, and in that of everyone, waiting to be resurrected there, so that he can share with us the divine life and love that circulates eternally in the Trinity.

5

REDEMPTION

Christ is the full expression of the Father. Jesus, the humanity of Christ, is the full manifestation of all that the Father is, insofar as this can be expressed in human nature. Jesus is the living symbol of God's love, mercy, and incredible tenderness toward his creatures. He is also the way that God communicates divine life to us. The actions that Christ performed during his earthly life expressed his inner dispositions, and none more completely than his passion, death, and resurrection, toward which the whole of his life was oriented. By knowing the historical Jesus, by listening to his Word in the Gospel and in the events of his life, we learn, little by little, to interiorize his teaching and his actions and begin to understand them. This is what we might call *deep listening.*

But like Mary of Bethany at the feet of Jesus, it is not enough just to listen to his words with our ears and to reflect on them with our reason. This is only an essential preliminary to getting acquainted with him, as in getting acquainted with any new friend. If we are really interested in making this friendship grow, we will find out all we can about him, spend time in prayer, and put his teaching into practice. As we reflect on the Word of God and the humanity of Jesus, we begin to listen with the ears of our hearts. Just as we can converse with someone on the level of words, so we can commune with someone on the level of silence. If we are quite closely acquainted, we can do it just by sitting together and communing without words. Anyone who has a close friend knows this experience.

But there is an even deeper level of conversation than communion, and that is *unity*. It is to this level that the Word of God is ultimately addressed. This is the capacity to listen with our whole being. Total response to Christ is only possible when we hear his word on every level of our being, including the deepest level, which is that of interior silence. It is at this level that his Word is most powerful and most creative; action that emerges from that silence is effective. And it is from this level that the apostle Paul speaks to us. Paul speaks frequently about participation in the life, passion and resurrection of Christ. His words are of special interest in that he is the one apostle who never knew the historical Jesus. Yet he was able to say, "It is no longer I that live, but Christ who lives in me" (Gal. 2:20).

As we have seen, there is a special view of time in the Christian perspective. The eternal, once it has fully entered into chronological time, as it did with the resurrection of Christ, has brought us what the scriptures call "the last times," or "the eighth day," which signifies the day after earthly time. Thus, a new kind of time has begun, one that includes both heaven and earth, the absolute and the relative, the eternal and the temporal. The kingdom of God is now reigning; that is, the values of eternal life, together with a real participation in them, are now present in those who believe in Jesus. These values are preserved in the Church, especially in the sacraments. The fact that the Church exists in a visible way is the sign that the grace of Christ is in the world, available to everyone at every moment of time. Our participation in the life of Christ is in direct proportion to our own growth in the eternal values which Jesus brought into the world and made permanently available through the sacraments, prayer, and fidelity to our conscience.

Paul says, "While we live, we are always being given up to death for Jesus' sake, so that the life of Jesus may be manifested in our mortal flesh" (2 Cor. 4:11). Thus, according to his view, the passion and resurrection of Christ are going on all the time. They are always present and not limited to an historical moment. It was rather an historical moment which introduced the eternal values of the cross and resurrection into the whole of time. We participate in Christ's divine life through baptism and the other sacraments. As a consequence, we must learn how to express the risen life of Jesus rather than our false selves in our conduct and relationships. To attain this union involves the transformation of our inmost being and all our faculties into the mind of Christ. This is the very fulness of salvation.

The chief expression of the mind of Christ is found in the classical text of Philippians: "Have this mind among yourselves, which you have in Christ Jesus, who, though he was in the form of God, did not count equality with God a thing to be grasped, but emptied himself, taking the form of a servant, being born in the likeness of men. And being found in human form, he humbled himself and became obedient unto death, even death on a cross" (Phil. 2:5-8).

God's great love recommends itself to us in this, that Christ gave up being God, so to speak, in order to become human. This is the "marvelous exchange" that the liturgy sings about at Christmastime. The Son of God regarded being God as secondary to the salvation of the human family. His purpose was not only to atone for our sins, but to take the whole human family with its incredible potential and its pathetic limitations to himself. He wants to flood the human family with the maximum degree of divine life that each of us is capable of receiving, and to gather us back into himself for the glory of the Father.

Today each of us has a unique capacity to express Christ to the people we meet. Each of us is called by God to be an incarnation of Christ, not in the sense that we become God through an absolute identity, but by becoming united to his Son, Jesus Christ. Christ, the Son of the Father, extends to each of us the same love which he has for his own human nature. The Father also extends to us, as brothers and sisters of Jesus Christ and members of his mystical body, the same infinite love which he has for his only-begotten Son.

6

SALVATION

The Christian message presupposes that we are sinners in a world needy of salvation. Paul puts the message in its most primitive form: "I delivered to you as of first importance what I also received, that Christ died for our sins in accordance with the scriptures; that he was buried; that he was raised on the third day in accordance with the scriptures; and that he appeared to Cephas, then to the twelve" (1 Cor. 15:3–5).

Salvation means not only having a change of heart in which one repents of having done evil. This is the beginning. But, like any beginning, one has to go on from there. Salvation is an ongoing process of growth. There is the salvation that comes when one initially accepts faith in Jesus Christ and is baptized. There is the more profound salvation that comes when one has developed the spiritual gifts given in baptism over the long course of a Christian life seriously pursued.

The Kingdom of God, Jesus said, "is like a grain of mustard seed" (Mark 4:31), the tiniest of seeds. The first stage of the process is to put the mustard seed into the ground where it germinates. Afterwards, it pushes a shoot through the earth and starts to grow. Later, it puts forth branches and leaves and becomes a tree. It is only at the end of the process, and not without a certain amount of pruning, that the tree bears fruit, and we observe with satisfaction that the seed has at last become something worthwhile. In similar fashion, the process of salvation is going on all the time, and although, for a Christian, it starts with faith in Jesus Christ and repentance, it has to go through a long period of growth before the follower of Christ becomes mature and "equipped for every good work" (2 Tim. 3:17).

The Christian idea of salvation has some similarities to the idea of liberation in the Eastern religions. All the religions of the world are in agreement about the *fact* that the human family is in a serious predicament, even if there are a variety of opinions as to how it got there. This predicament is identified by a need for escape from the circle of ever-recurring evil habits with their ensuing misery. The Christian tradition regards the cure of this malaise as a return to intimacy with God, which is the source of human wholeness. This intimacy was lost to the human race through a corporate fault symbolized by the story of the fall of Adam and Eve, called original sin.

Whether you think that the restoration of this intimacy has to take place over many lives, or simply in one lifetime, everybody agrees that it has to be done. According to all the great religions of the world, the essential work of every human life is to prepare for union with the ultimate reality.

We believe, as Christians, that Jesus Christ, by means of his sacrificial suffering and death on the cross, brought salvation and liberation to the whole world. At the same time, we believe that Christ's passion, death, and resurrection is an eternal event. Just because it happened in chronological time does not mean that anyone — past, present, or future — is excluded from its benefits. In this connection, the Catholic Church teaches that it was in view of the *foreseen* merits of Christ that Mary was preserved from the limitations of original sin. In other words, because of the redeeming death of Christ, but *before* it took place, Mary received the unique grace of coming into the world without the limitations of original sin.

In the account of creation and the fall in the Book of Genesis, the first man and woman were promised a savior. Revelation thus teaches that the grace of salvation was always present in the world because God intended in chronological time to sacrifice his only-begotten Son to guarantee it. The only way that he could sacrifice his Son was by allowing him to assume a human nature which could suffer and die. From the beginning of time all who were saved and sanctified have received whatever grace they have received through the redeeming death of the Son of God. His sacrifice is an eternal event, and its fruits are available at every point of time.

Paul says that anyone who truly seeks God, believing that God will reward him, will receive the gift of grace. In other words, when anyone follows his conscience, in which the law of God is written, at some point he will meet the grace of Christ, since it is offered to everyone of good will. Whether he knows the historical Jesus or not, he will come to know Christ as the eternal Word of God, the Cosmic Christ, who "enlightens everyone" (John 1:9) and through whom "all things were made" (John 1:3). He will come to know the Christ who is in the inmost conscience of every man and woman, waiting to manifest himself to them in the degree that they follow the promptings of their conscience. Whoever attains to grace, attains the grace of Christ.

The great gift which Christ won through his sacrificial death is intimacy and oneness with the Father. On the day of his resurrection he said triumphantly to Mary Magdalene, "Go to my brethren and say to them that I am ascending to my Father and *your* Father" (John 20:17). That is the great good news! The experience of intimacy with God, symbolized in Genesis by God's daily walk with Adam and Eve in the evening air (Gen. 3:8), is now available once again to the whole human family.

The gates of heaven closing after Adam and Eve is a vivid symbol of the ripe fruits of original sin, which are man's alienation from God and from himself. Adam and Eve lost what they were intended to have, namely, intimacy with God, which is the only true source of security. When intimacy with God was gone, they and their progeny could only search for security "down the labyrinthine ways of time."*

Christ's coming and his sacrifice have taken away the guilt of all men and women, so that the capacity to return to the state of human wholeness has been made accessible to the entire human family regardless of time. God chose to atone for the sin of the world by sending his own Son, who on account of his divine dignity, could release the human family not only from any amount of guilt that it had or might incur, but at the same time catapult it into the possibility of a higher level of intimacy with God than it had before.

---

*Francis Thompson, "The Hound of Heaven," in *The World's Great Catholic Poetry*, ed. Thomas Walsh (New York: Macmillan, 1947), p. 327.

7

FAITH

Faith is the essential means of attaining salvation. We cannot reach faith by reasoning. It is like an intuition. We can prepare for it by reflection, by longing for it, and by pleading for it. But it can only come as a gift. Once it has been given, life assumes a new direction. A Christian is like someone getting on an elevator. Such a person is not interested in going anywhere horizontally; his desire is to go up.

If we conceptualize the Christian life as an ascent toward God, getting on an elevator for the first time and closing the door is an act of faith. We do not know what will happen. The door may open on the second, third, or fourth floor and, to our amazement, we find a new perspective of the world stretching out before us. After having enjoyed the vista on one floor, we get back on the elevator and enter once again into darkness. We have to make a new act of faith in order to get to the next level; that is, we have to go through the pain of passing through the transition from one level to the next.

Faith is not just the assent of our minds to a series of dogmas.

Such a superficial view drains it of its full meaning. Faith is basically the surrender of our will. It is not a matter of understanding with our heads; it is the gift of our entire being to God — to the ultimate reality. It orients us definitively in his direction.

Here is another example. Suppose a neighbor's house starts to burn down. His little boy is trapped on the third floor while all the rest of the family have escaped. The father cannot go back into the house to rescue him. He is standing outside under the window and sees him at the window, silhouetted against the flames. He cries out, "Jump! I'll catch you!" The little boy's eyes are filled with smoke, so he cannot see his father or the ground. He is afraid to jump, even though he desperately wants to be saved. The father cries out again, "Jump! Don't be afraid!"

The little boy cries out: "But Daddy, I can't see you!"

The father calls back: "But I see you! Jump!" So the youngster climbs out onto the window sill and jumps. He lands safely in his father's outstretched arms.

This parable points to what faith is. Of course, most of us have yet to arrive in our Father's arms. We are still in our free fall.

By jumping out of the window, we choose a direction, where we want to go; that is, into the arms of God, whom we firmly believe is waiting to enfold us. The condition is that we trust him. As soon as we begin to want to see and understand, or to depend on concepts or feelings to go to God, we withdraw from faith. Faith calls for the total surrender of our faculties and of all our being to the truth inside and outside ourselves. The Christian tradition calls this reality God.

Christian faith is a leap into the unknown. Experience confirms the wisdom of every act of trust. The alternation of the darkness of faith leading to understanding, and understanding illuminating the darkness of faith is the normal way that leads to the growth of faith. Like everyone else, God wants to be accepted as he is — and he happens to be infinite, incomprehensible, inexpressible. We have to accept him, then, in the darkness of faith. It is only when we can accept God as he is that we can give up the desire for spiritual experiences that we can feel. Faith is mature when we are at ease without particular experiences of God, when his presence is obvious without our having to reflect on it. One who has this faith simply opens his eyes and, wherever he looks, finds God.

Faith is strengthened by reading and meditation on the Word of God, prayer, fidelity to the duties of our state of life, and the acceptance of the circumstances of life. We must try to perceive Christ in the interruption of our plans and in the disappointment of our expectations; in difficulties, contradictions, and trials. No matter what happens, "We know that in everything God works for good with those who love him" (Rom. 8:28). The Holy Spirit works on our evolution not only by purifying and enlightening us from within, but also by allowing difficulties, trials, and temptations to assail us from without. This much is certain, that once we make up our minds to seek God, he is already seeking us much more eagerly, and he is not going to let anything happen to prevent his purpose. He will bring people and events into our lives, and whatever we may think about them, they are designed for the evolution of his life in us.

8

LECTIO DIVINA

There is a great difference between theological speculation on the truths of faith and faith itself. As Christians, we have to interiorize the truths of faith, so that we can understand them at the level of the heart as well as at the level of the mind.

Lectio divina has a long tradition in the Christian church which was brought to full bloom in the monasteries during the Middle Ages. This Latin term literally means *divine reading*. The practice involves the reading of scripture as a divinely in- spired message. It is, therefore, a special way of reading scrip- ture. It is, above all, an exercise of faith, attentiveness, and self- surrender. It is not done with a view to exegesis, nor to research- ing the historical background of the text nor the philological roots of the words. Those scientific disciplines are very helpful to get at the literal meaning of the Word of God in scripture. But *lectio divina* is neither a study nor a science. Its purpose is not information, but insight. It is a very creative kind of reading. It is a sacred art, and like any art, requires discipline and a long apprenticeship.

The model for this kind of reading is provided by the liturgy, which, as it evolved in the early Christian church, became what might be called *applied scripture*; the practical application of the meaning of scripture to spiritual growth and the challenges of daily life. The mystery of Christ unfolds during the course of the major feasts and seasons of the liturgical year, as it focuses on the events of Christ's life, death, and resurrection. The liturgy is a totally comprehensive pedagogical program, teaching moral, dogmatic, ascetical, and mystical theology all at the same time and in an existential manner. Through the grace of Christ's abiding presence in the sacraments, the liturgy communicates inwardly what it commemorates outwardly in the sacred rites and celebrations of the Church.

The model for *lectio divina* provided by the liturgy is the action of listening to the Word of God and responding. We can only respond to something that really impresses us. The more deeply something affects us, the more completely it engages our faculties and energies, and the more profound and permanent our response is likely to be.

In the study of speculative theology and in the scientific study of scripture, a great many values are obtained, but they are all on the same level, the level of the intellect. That is fine as far as it goes, but it does not go far enough. If theology is taught only as one more science among many, the preaching of the Gospel will become sterile indeed. Even the study of scripture can become as dry as dust if the scientific approach is the only point of view the students are learning. Moreover, this approach to scripture can leave students wilted instead of inspired. This is a serious problem for seminaries today. Although they have rightly responded to the demand for scientific excellence required by our times, the education they impart is too much on the level of reasoning. The great truths that are being communicated to the heads of the students are not getting through to their hearts.

Archbishop Fulton J. Sheen used to say that in secular universities knowledge went from the notebook of the professor into the notebook of the student without passing through the minds of either. In seminaries today there is danger that the knowledge of theology and scripture may pass through the minds of the professors into the minds of the students without passing through the hearts of either. Unless it finds a place in their hearts, the message of the Gospel may be preached, but it is not going to be lived. The Gospel is addressed to the *whole* man, body, mind, and heart. Christian practice requires an integral approach to the Gospel. This involves study, of course, but also the effective assimilation of the truths of faith through discursive meditation, affective prayer, contemplation, and love of the person of Jesus Christ.

Christianity is not centered around a moral teaching, but around a person — one who is both man and God at the same time — two natures indissolubly linked in the oneness of a single person. The scripture is the normal way of introducing us gradually to the knowledge and love of this person. This process involves the kind of dynamic that happens in making friends with anybody. You have to spend time together, talk together, listen to each other, and get to know each other. At first you feel a little awkward and strange in one another's company, but as you get better acquainted, and especially as you begin to feel yourself going out to the goodness you perceive in each other, the amount of time spent in conversation begins to diminish. You are at ease to rest in one another's presence with just a happy sense of well-being.

The process that I have spoken of in terms of human friendship is the way *lectio divina* works too. In a sense, it is a methodless way of meditation. It does not depend on some particular technique, but on the natural evolution of friendship. *Lectio divina* is a time that one spends on a regular basis with the Word of God in scripture. It is a personal exchange. The Cistercian monks of the 12th century normally spent three hours every day in *lectio divina*, and longer at certain times of the year when manual labor was less demanding.

Lectio divina in the monastic setting was supported by an atmosphere of silence and solitude and a routine conducive to recollection. It was interspersed with periods of pslamody and chanting, which put the monks in a frame of mind helpful for reflection and calm. When the mind is not agitated by many thoughts, it can settle down rather quickly into a synthesis of what one has been reading or thinking. Without such supportive structure, people usually need a technique in order to enter into the kind of interior silence that is necessary for deep listening to the word of God.

A practical method of preparing for *lectio* is probably necessary in our contemporary world, which is so full of input from television, radio, and printed material. We are bombarded by all kinds of impressions, propaganda, and advertising all day long. Moreover, one cannot go immediately from haste, conflict, or anxiety into a state of attentiveness without some preparation. Practicing some form of meditation or technique for quieting the mind, saying a few psalms, reciting part of the Rosary, praying in tongues if one has the gift, or even some brief relaxation exercises, could help. The fruitfulness of *lectio divina* presupposes a certain calmness of mind when we come to it. Good sense would at least suggest using a regular time for *lectio divina* when we are fully awake, but before the cares of the day have gotten entrenched in our minds. Then, by reading a few pages of scripture, a few paragraphs, or perhaps only a few words, we find ourselves in the presence of God, our Father, our friend — this extraordinary person we are trying to know. We need to listen eagerly to his words, applying our whole being to them. This is the reason why the ancient custom was to read aloud, or at least to form the words on one's lips, so that the body, too, entered into the process.

The Holy Spirit inspired those who wrote the scriptures. He is also in our hearts inspiring us and teaching us how to read and listen. When these two inspirations fuse, we really understand what scripture is saying; or at least we understand what God at this moment is saying to us through it. This insight is not just an abstract reflection; it bears on our conduct. It usually speaks to our hearts. It may also suggest some concrete action: "Should I give up a certain attitude?. . . Should I make a greater effort to reach out to someone?" Since the inspiration of the Holy Spirit is a recommendation of his, we have confidence that he will help us to carry it out.

Lectio divina is like the experience of the disciples on the road to Emmaus (Luke 24:13-26). They were walking away from Jerusalem in a mood of great distress and discouragement — not good dispositions for *lectio divina*. Jesus came along hiding his identity at first, and asked them, "What is on your minds?" (Luke 24:17). When they related their inner turmoil, he began to explain the passages of scripture that referred to his passion and death. This is the discursive part of *lectio divina*, the careful reflection on what is actually said in the text. It was during this time that their hearts began to burn. When they reflected on the encounter later, they said to each other, "Were not our hearts burning when the Lord spoke to us on the road and *explained* the scriptures to us?" (Luke 24:32). It is the Holy Spirit, the Spirit of Christ, dwelling in our hearts, who explains the meaning of scripture when we try to understand it, not as a science, not in order to teach others, but simply as a means of communing with God.

Once Christ had prepared the disciples by opening up the deeper meaning of scripture and by awakening an ardent longing for him in their hearts, they were ready to celebrate the

Eucharist. They invited him to accompany them as they entered the inn. He sat down with them and broke bread. It was at this moment that "their eyes were opened" (Luke 24:31). This was the moment of blinding insight, in which Christ, who had been hidden from them in the form of a stranger, suddenly became transparent to the eyes of their faith. They penetrated his human presence to the divine person who had always been there, but who for the first time they really saw and perceived with a living faith. This experience turned their lives around, and they went straight back to Jerusalem in haste to share their new-found enthusiasm with the other disciples. All the anxieties which had caused them to run away had disappeared instantly through the recognition of the presence of Christ. They were ready to bear witness to him without hesitation, and to live out of that experience.

Each period of *lectio divina* follows the same plan: reflection on the Word of God, followed by free expression of the spontaneous feelings that arise in our hearts. The whole gamut of human response to truth, beauty, goodness, and love is possible. As the heart reaches out in longing for God, it begins to penetrate the words of the sacred text. Mind and heart are united and rest in the presence of Christ. *Lectio divina* is a way of meditation that leads naturally to spontaneous prayer, and little by little, to moments of contemplation — to insights into the Word of God and the deeper meaning and significance of the truths of faith. This activity enables us to be nourished by the "bread of life" (John 6:35), and indeed to *become* the Word of God (John 6:48-51).

9

PRAYER

Prayer is a large umbrella. There are many kinds of prayer and many ways of expressing it. Fundamentally, it is a response to God's invitation to turn our minds and hearts to him. The classical formulas are that of Evagrius, which is the laying aside of thoughts; and that of St. John Damascene, which is conversation of the mind with God. By "mind" St. John means the spiritual faculties of intellect and will. Sometimes this interior movement needs to be expressed in words or concepts, but to be true prayer, it does not have to be expressed by words or concepts.

The Fathers of the Church and the great spiritual masters of the Christian tradition have elaborated on various levels and degrees of prayer. We may also think of prayer as a conversation with God, which deepens as one becomes more and more devoted to him. That deepening does not prevent us from expressing prayer spontaneously on every level of our being, from the spoken word of prayer to the simple movement of the will, which the *Cloud of Unknowing* calls a "gentle stirring of love."* This simple movement of the will is scarcely perceptible to our attention, but at the deepest level of our being, it unites us more intimately to the Holy Spirit than any other form of prayer. For, as St. John of the Cross teaches, the Spirit is the sole mover at that deep level of interior silence and works powerfully without our being aware of what is happening.† To arrive at that state of contemplative prayer, some preliminary activity is required.

Contemplative prayer can greatly benefit from some method of improving our capacity for interior silence. One reason for this is the nature of our cultural climate. In the West, the analytical approach to knowledge has been pushed to its utmost limits. It has produced wonderful advances in science. But when it comes to prayer and interior silence, Western man is somewhat embarrassed and ill at ease. He needs to cultivate his intuitive capacities. That is why some method conducive to contemplative prayer could put a little order into his efforts and hasten the result.

Make no mistake about it: there is no instantaneous contemplation. However, a method for overcoming our habitual inclination to rely too much on concepts in going to God during the time of prayer could be extremely helpful. One such method is suggested in the *Cloud of Unknowing*. St. John of the Cross suggests another when he describes the movement from discursive meditation to a more simplified and contemplative form of prayer.‡ It is important to realize that in this movement God's action is more important than ours. Any method or technique is only a predisposition, a way of removing obstacles or of undoing habits of mind which are a hindrance to contemplation.

*William Johnston, ed., *The Cloud of Unknowing* (Garden City, N.Y.: Doubleday, 1973), p. 48.

†St. John of the Cross, *Living Flame of Love*, trans. E. Allison Peers (Garden City, N.Y.: Doubleday, 1971) Stanza III, 58.

‡St. John of the Cross, *Living Flame of Love*, Stanza III, 26-58.

Through this process we become better instruments, or, to use the Gospel image, soil that is better prepared to receive the seed of God's word. God's word is meant to take possession of all our faculties and to bring about our gradual transformation into Christ. Therefore, we act out of his world view and his consciousness, rather than out of our own narrow, ego-centered consciousness.

Eastern methods of developing interior silence seem to overlook certain stages of preparation which the Christian tradition has emphasized, namely, the practice of discursive meditation and affective prayer. Apart from any method, some people are overtaken spontaneously by the gift of God. He dwells within us and can reach up any time and pull us down to where he dwells in an encounter of deep interior silence and peace. He can also come forth and invade our everyday consciousness with his overwhelming presence. But normally he does not exercise these initiatives, or at least not very often. That is why methods or preparing the soil of the soul for the Word of God are normally necessary for intimate contact with him on a regular or continuous basis.

Those who have experienced the peace that emerges out of deep interior silence through some Eastern technique will be disinclined toward a conceptual form of prayer. They will ask, "What is wrong with what I am doing? If I make use of words or concepts, I feel that I am treating God as an object, while in my method of meditation, I seem to experience God at a much deeper level of my being." This is a nice problem to have. At the same time, from the perspective of integrating our entire human nature and giving it to God, we need to have contact with God in more than one way, even if we believe our one way is the best way. Contemplative prayer does, in fact, put all other forms of prayer in proper perspective.

The Christian tradition presents contemplation and the rest

of interior silence as the result of much effort devoted to purifying the mind and heart and to replacing old habits of thinking and acting with new ones. This process generally takes a long time. However, we must not overdo this teaching. Paul exhorts us to take for granted that we have already received as a pure gift in baptism all that we need in order to attain salvation by virtue of Christ's passion, death, and resurrection. We have only to enter by faith into the kingdom that has already been established in the depth of our spirit and take possession of it.

Thus, if we truly give ourselves to God in faith and open our minds and hearts to him, we may begin to find him in the silence of the prayer of faith very quickly. The prayer of faith is an approach to God without concepts. It is to accept God as he is, in the way he presents himself to us in the scripture, impossible to contain in any concept, but not impossible to contact through the love of self-surrender. By means of the regular practice of the prayer of faith, the vestibule to contemplative prayer is gradually established. It is in that silence that the infused virtues and gifts of the Spirit are greatly strengthened and developed.

Suppose we as Christians have entered into an experience of interior silence through an Eastern meditative practice without any reflection on the Christian truths.

There will be an apparent dichotomy between the spiritual experience we have through one of these methods and the truths that we received on an abstract level when we were instructed in the Christian religion at Sunday school. We may wonder whether these two can be put together. Yet, if our background is in the Christian tradition, we need to put them together. Otherwise, they are going to keep rolling around in our psyche like bowling balls heading in opposite directions.

We should realize that in God's loving kindness and providence for us, he has given us a way of entering into interior silence and becoming acquainted with our own spiritual nature. That gives us a head start on many Christians, who even though they were instructed intellectually in the faith, have not really interiorized Christian values through a regular method of prayer and the practice of virtue.

It is important for those who have experienced this peace to realize that, at the very least, it is an experience of their own spiritual nature. Moreover, if they have been baptized, that is to say, sealed in a real but spiritual way by the grace of Christ, any kind of meditation that leads to interior silence easily becomes a prayer.

When a Christian tries to extract one of the physical or psychic disciplines from an Eastern tradition and introduce it into his own religious pracitce, the question has to be asked: Can one graft a branch from one kind of fruit tree onto the trunk of another and expect to produce the same fruit as the new trunk? What actually happens is that the branch that is grafted onto the new trunk will indeed continue to bear fruit, but fruit of the kind from which it came. What effect will this grafting have on our growth as Christians?

Much work has to be done to make the similarities between the spiritualities of the East and Christianity understood, let alone available, to the average person. This will require not only an intensive study of the spiritual disciplines of other religious cultures, but also a firm grasp of one's own. A great deal of experience and dialogue is presupposed in order to understand correctly what the terms of another religious culture really mean, as well as what the long-range effects of a bodily discipline may be on the psyche of a person from a different culture.

On a modest level, however, there are some immediate benefits to be gained from certain disciplines of the East, even if they are separated from their conceptual background. For instance, the sitting posture of Zen Buddhism is unquestionably one of the most relaxed postures that has ever been discovered, and it has been proven to have a remarkably quieting effect upon the mind. There is no reason why this posture could not be incorporated into our Christian prayer without further concern. It is a posture which allows prayer to be prolonged without moving, a point that St. Ignatius singles out as important in the *Spiritual Exercises.** He presents a series of optional positions to the meditator, but he specifies one condition — that whatever posture is chosen, it is to be maintained without change throughout the whole meditation period.

It is not necessary to add the dimension of particular beliefs to benefit from a specific practice like Zen sitting. But a good understanding of the conceptual background of the practice is desirable, if that can be integrated into our Christian understanding, too.

In Zen Buddhism, the sitting position is based on the firm conviction that everyone possesses Buddha nature; that by sitting, the mind and the body will gradually be integrated; and that the reality of Buddha nature will eventually rise to full awareness once the mind is thoroughly quieted. This belief corresponds to the Christian teaching that the Holy Trinity dwells at the center of our spirit. Thus, a similar kind of conviction is presupposed by this posture, whether one is a Zen Buddhist or a Christian.

A thoroughgoing return to the sources of Christian spirituality could serve two important purposes: (1) to know more fully our own spiritual tradition so that we can renew it and re-express it in our time (this has to be the first step) and (2) to be challenged by the insights of Eastern spirituality, perhaps even to integrate them into our Christian tradition. And those who are steeped in the Christian tradition are the best qualified to make excursions into Eastern thought and practice.

---

*The Spiritual Exercises of St. Ignatius, trans. Louis Puhl (Chicago: Loyola University Press, 1951), First Week, Additions 4, p. 36.

While the disciplines of the East bring to the spiritual journey values which are complementary to the spiritual traditions of Christianity, especially the understanding of how the body enters into the spiritual journey, the Christian tradition also has much to offer to the East — above all, the conviction of God's unbounded love for each human being, which in turn summons us not only to respond to him, but to the needs of all humanity, both individual and social. The specific work of integrating the respective values of each tradition is waiting to be accomplished.

Meanwhile, many Christians have turned to the East today because the experience of the transcendent is lacking in the various denominations in which they were raised. Many have also turned away from their churches because an overly strict interpretation of its moral teachings was foisted upon them at a time when they were too young to understand them or to integrate them into the love of God. As a result, words associated with the Christian religion like faith, sin, and salvation, have overtones that many contemporary Christians cannot endure. From among these two categories of alienated Christians, significant numbers have been instructed in an Eastern meditation technique that has done them a lot of good. The technique succeeded in interesting them initially because it was presented in terminology that they were not reacting against. At some point, however, as a result of the more disciplined life which the technique required, they are sufficiently open to spiritual values to feel an attraction to return to the faith of their childhood. The experience of spiritual values brings them closer to Christ. If somebody could show them how the spiritual experience they found in their Eastern method of meditation corresponds to experiences which are normal for a Christian also, this would give them tremendous encouragement, and enable them to consider the possibility of continuing their spiritual journey in the framework of their early religious background.

Unfortunately, many people who have sought to return to their Christian roots have not been well received in their local parishes. Thus, they have felt rejected at the very moment when they were ready to return to the Church. Their enriching experience could have been easily articulated in terms of Christian spirituality. But they found no one to show them how to relate their Eastern experience to their Christian background.

10

INTERIOR SILENCE

Prayer can be expressed in words, thoughts, or acts of the will. But fundamentally it is a movement of our spiritual nature; that is, of our intellect beyond thoughts and of our will beyond particular acts—at least beyond explicit acts. This movement toward God can be extremely subtle and delicate. The more simple it is, the more effective it is. It can be a wordless turning or opening of our awareness to God, whom we know is present. We do not have to conceptualize *how* he is present, because we really do not know. When as Christians, we enter into deep interior silence and our thoughts are "laid aside," as Evagrius puts it, and we have gone beyond the imagination and its working, where are we? It seems the only place we can possibly be is in our spirit; and since Christ dwells at the center of our spirit, we, as baptized Christians, may be coming closer to experiencing him, even without explicitly intending it. Should we continue to practice our interior silence on a regular basis, something of the radiance of his presence will begin to dawn on us. This shouldn't surprise us. It may express itself in an attraction to return to our Christian background, if we had one, or to incarnate our experience by introducing a religious expression into our life.

It might be even more explicit. We may begin to be aware that God, the Word made flesh, is dwelling at the very center of our being. In any case, the movement toward interior silence triggers a phenomenon that might be called centering. St. John of the Cross has a few words about this that are enlightening. He says that we are attracted to God as to our center, like a stone toward the center of the earth. If we remove the obstacles, the ego-self with all its paraphernalia, and surrender to God, we penetrate through the various layers of our psyche until we reach the very center or core of our being. At that point there remains one more center to which we may advance. This center is the Trinity, Father, Son, and Holy Spirit, who dwell at the inmost center of our being. It is out of that Presence that our whole being emerges at every moment. To be at this center is eternal life. To remain at this center in the midst of activity is what Christ called the reign of God.*

Once we are thoroughly established in interior silence, it accompanies or pursues us through our daily routine. While conversations with God on other levels will still arise spontaneously, interior silence is the essential conversation. However, because we are human, we need to conceptualize and express that experience. There must be a conceptual framework in order to verbalize and share this wonderful life with other people; and for a Christian that conceptual framework has to be a Christian framework. It is like learning a trade. By exercising a trade, we benefit other people and gain great satisfaction for ourselves. Every faculty is designed to enjoy its own exercise. So it is in the spiritual life. There is nothing more delightful than being con-

---

*St. John of the Cross, *Living Flame of Love* (Garden City, N.Y.: Doubleday, 1971), Stanza I, 12.

cretely spiritual. Still, communion with God must be integrated into all the levels of our being so that this communion is experienced, not only on the level of interior silence, but on the level of thought, feelings, and action. Thus, if a Christian is meditating in the sense of transcending, he or she should at other times read and ponder the scriptures, trying to interiorize the word of God and conceptualize it, so that the word heard inwardly in silence is confirmed by the word heard outwardly. These two "words" are not contradictory. They are complementary and form one whole. They balance and reinforce each other. Thus, a Christian avoids falling into excessive subjectivity or excessive objectivity. Moreover, he or she will know how to express and stabilize the spiritual experiences thus received.

This is an important point. One young man I knew was in great anguish because he was having spiritual experiences of a profound character, but nothing in his religious training had given him any way of verbalizing them. He was like a man who was tongue-tied. He desperately wanted to find out whether his experiences were true or not. The only way he could recognize what he was talking about was through the expressions of negativity that he was using. This was a good indication that his spiritual experience had come to that level of deep faith that cannot be conceptualized. But his particular Christian background had not prepared him for that experience.

There are a lot of Christians, as well as other people, roaming about in the world today, who experience the unexpected invasion of God's presence every now and then, but do not know what to make of it. It can be scary. They are even more scared to tell their friends for fear they might be told, "You must be nuts. Better go see a psychiatrist."

In any case, Christians who are experiencing interior silence need to have a Christian conceptual frame of reference. There is one. If we can get acquainted with it, we will feel much more at ease, because we will be able to express our experience in terms of our faith. Even though we feel more at home at that silent level of communication with God, we will not be constricted in expressing it in other forms when these are appropriate. We will feel ill at ease at religious services that are superficial, perfunctory, and which do not provide adequate opportunities for silence, but faith must triumph over these human limitations. The Christian religion must be presented as a process of spiritual growth, an interior evolution toward eternal values which are to be experienced to an extraordinary degree here and now. Otherwise, the Gospel is not being preached in its entirety.

Unfortunately, human limitations have too often prevailed over the presentation of the Gospel in its entirety. The purity and simplicity of the Gospel have been diluted by the inroads of the secular culture, with its almost exclusive emphasis on analysis and on the use of technology in order to dominate nature, the world, and other people. Yet, it is at just this present moment that the world is on the threshold of a great spiritual confrontation between the East and Christianity. This confrontation could be one of the greatest moments in history. Never before have the Vedic and Buddhist traditions confronted the Christian tradition on so broad a scale. Unfortunately, what they are confronting is not Christianity in its primitive unity, but forms of Christianity which have been debilitated by four centuries of division among the various denominations, and by the consequences of the analytical approach.

The analytical approach can be very good in developing one aspect of the human potential. It has led to the advantages of the technological age, most of which we enjoy. Yet, it also has had the effect of stifling our intuitive faculties, at least in their contemplative dimension. It has made Western culture very onesided. Apart from a few geniuses, the intuitive side of most men, and I suppose of most women too, has been truncated. And now, with the burgeoning interest developing in the values of transcendent experience, many Christians are unaware of the fact that their own tradition is rich in spirituality and mystical wisdom. Christian mysticism was highly developed in previous centuries and can be called upon at this time, both to understand the Christian experience and the spiritual traditions of the East.

Where are we to learn these truths? A good start would be to take steps to provide adequate training in seminaries so that priests and ministers would be able to understand and transmit them. There are historical reasons why training in the area of spirituality has not been adequate. In the not-too-far-distant past, the general teaching in seminaries and novitiates was that one would be guilty of presumption or might even endanger his salvation, if he practiced anything but discursive meditation. The impression was given that it was almost better not to pray at all than to practice contemplative prayer. While this situaion has greatly improved, much work still remains to be done in novitiates and seminaries to renew the traditional spiritual teaching of the Church. Preaching the Gospel will never come to life unless priests, ministers, and seminarians, early in their training, have a profound awareness that Christianity is a life to be lived — an interior life that is incredibly rewarding and which has marvellous potential for development and growth. They cannot reach the fulness of their vocation without growing in interior prayer and spiritual development; nor can they make the Gospel alive for others without the gift of wisdom, which penetrates the meaning of scripture and grasps what Christ is actually saying. Today large numbers of people are looking for gennuine spirituality, and unless they find it articulated precisely where they are — on the parish level or on college campuses — they will just go down the street in search of someplace else.

There should be a center of Christian spirituality somewhere in every diocese — a place where people who are well instructed in prayer are available. Clergy who do not have special training or the necessary experience could then refer people to these places. Such centers might also be places where people trained in Eastern practices could be helped to integrate this knowledge into a Christian frame of reference.

Without the presentation of the contemplative dimension of the Christian religion, the Gospel is not being fully proclaimed, because the most important part of it is being left out. Until now, Christianity has made next to no inroads in the East because it did not bring the contemplative dimension of Christianity to peoples whose traditions are profoundly contemplative.

11

PRAYER AND EUCHARIST

Regarding the effectiveness of our prayer, we have to be careful not to project our own judgment on God. God responds to each of us where we are, and takes into account what we are capable of. Everyone of good will who offers prayer of any kind is certainly going to be heard. We do not have to wait until we have reached deep interior silence in order to pray. We must do the best we can and hope for the mercy of God. It is precisely by praying as well as we can that God is moved to raise us to a higher state of prayer. After all, the fundamental purpose of prayer, including the prayer of petition, is not to get something from God, or to change God, but to change ourselves. When *we* have changed, God can give us everything we want, because our wills will be one with his, and we will want only what he wants.

We pray in order to give ourselves to God, to become capable of receiving God, and to make it possible for God to do what he always wanted to do in the first place, which is to give us himself. Prayer is the condition that God is waiting for in order to communicate his divine life and holiness to us. Such is the purpose of his creating us in the first place.

There is an important connection between vocal prayer and the experience of interior silence. The Word of God emerges from the infinite silence of the Father, who is the source of the divine life. That is the model for every Christian life. When our own words and actions (which are also words) emerge from deep interior silence, we will begin to see spontaneously what is more important and what is less important in our daily occupations and duties. That will save us a lot of time in the long run.

In the liturgy, for instance, if the service itself began with a few moments of silence and ended with silence, or if the readings were preceded and followed by silent pauses, the experience of the sacred words emerging out of silence would be much more powerful and effective. It would make the hymns of praise and the prayers of petition much more meaningful to the congregation. There is an essential relationship between silence and speech, because everything comes out of silence. When our life emerges from periods of silence, it is a more genuine life; and when we return to silence, our life receives its truest meaning. In the beginning , both cannot be done at the same time, but in time they will tend to merge. Then, interior silence does not have to be prolonged in order to produce its good effects.

One of the things that prayer, as it deepens, will affect is our intuition of the oneness of the human race, and, indeed, the oneness of all creation. As one moves into his own inmost being, he comes into contact with what is the inmost being of everyone else. Although each of us retains his own unique personhood, we are necessarily associated with the God-man, who has taken the whole human family to himself in such a way as to be the inmost reality of each individual member of it. And so, when one is praying in the spirit, in his inmost being, one is praying, so to speak, in everybody else's spirit.

In the Eucharist, we are not only joined to Christ, whom we believe is present with his whole being under the symbols of bread and wine, but we believe that we are joined with all other Christians, with every member of the human race, and with the whole of creation. Christ is in the hearts of all men and women and in the heart of all creation, sustaining everything in being. This mystery of oneness enables us to emerge from the Eucharist with a refined inward eye, and invites us to perceive the mystery of Christ everywhere and in everything. He who is hidden from our senses and intellect becomes more and more transparent to the eyes of faith — to the consciousness that is being transformed. The Spirit in us perceives the Spirit in others. The Eucharist is the celebration of life, the dance of the divine in human form. We are part of that dance. Each of us is a continuation of Christ's incarnation, insofar as we are living Christ's life in our own lives — or rather, *instead of* our own lives. The Eucharist is the summary of all creation coming together in a single hymn of praise, surrender, and thanksgiving. In the Eucharist all creation is transformed into the body of Christ, transformed again into his divine person, and thrust into the depths of the Father for ever and ever. Even material creation has become divine in him. "For the creation," says Paul, "waits with eager longing for the revealing of the sons of God" (Rom. 8:19).

Prayer and interior silence deepen our appreciation of and receptivity to the Eucharist. The Eucharist also helps to develop and nourish prayer and interior silence. They are mutually reinforcing. Through deep prayer, one appreciates the meaning of the sacraments and increases their effectiveness.

It is not so much the length of time that one spends in interior silence, but the quality of it that is transforming, and that nourishes and refreshes at the deepest level. The most effective silence takes place when one is not even aware of being silent — when one has merged and lost his own identity in the mystery of

Christ. This union is the ultimate goal of the Eucharist. Interior union with Christ comes by assimilating the Eucharistic food into our own body and spirit. The bodily eating is the symbol of what is happening spiritually. It points to the interpenetration that is taking place between Christ and us. This interpenetration is designed to further our evolution into vertical time and our assimilation of the eternal values that Christ has brought into the world through his incarnation and communicated to us by his passion, death, resurrection, and ascension. The purpose of our historical lifetime is to provide us with space to complete this inward journey.

12

HUMILITY OF HEART

Humility is an attitude of honesty toward all reality. It is not self-depreciation, which is a neurotic tendency, but the truth. It is the conviction of being created out of nothing and of being gratuitously redeemed. Those are the two theological principles on which true humility, in the Christian sense, is based.

Reflect a moment on the way a newborn child begins to experience reality. As it looks around at things, it does not distinguish one from another. It does not know the difference between fire and water until it tries them out. It does not prefer something beautiful to something ugly, because it has not yet started to analyze the difference. It enjoys the *act* of seeing and does not worry about *what* it is seeing. This great art of enjoying the very *act* of seeing without distinguishing *what* is seen is a quality of the enjoyment of reality that God means us to retain all our life long. This does not mean, of course, that we cannot also begin to distinguish and analyze, but we should not distinguish and analyze so much that we can no longer enjoy the simple pleasures of life, such as those which emerge from the very act of doing them. The educational process in Western culture makes sure that we lose this basic and primeval kind of enjoyment as soon as possible by creating in us the need and desire to analyze everything — to reduce all experience to logic, cause and effect relationships, utility, efficiency, and profit.

Humility of heart is the capacity *just to be* for the sake of God. He called us into being. What more could one ask than the enjoyment of it? We did not ask for it; we did nothing to attain it. It *is*; and yet we cannot fully enjoy it without humility of heart. We always want to know, "What am I going to do with this being? Do I like it or don't I?" We are able to ask this question because we are free to be. And that freedom is what distinguishes us from the rest of material creation.

One way of entering into this fundamental Christian attitude is to learn once again what it means *just to be* — to allow ourselves to rest before God with the being he gave us, with no other intention, effort, or purpose, except to surrender that being back to him. This is the orientation of contemplative prayer and the ultimate purpose of every genuine spiritual exercise. Our part is to prepare our faculties to become interiorly quiet until thoughts about God are no longer as important to us as the mystery of God's presence. Our part is to identify with that deep pervasive peace, and not to want to do anything else — not even to brush away the superficial distractions that pass through our mind. This orientation of contemplative prayer is the closest thing to the experience of being, short of God's drawing us into union with himself. We cannot bring this union about, but we can prepare ourselves to receive it, by learning again *just to be* before God.

Humility of heart is not only *just to be*. It is also the spontaneous capacity *just to do*. One cannot *just do* until he has first learned *just to be*. It is out of that experience of *just being* that one can then be content with the joy of *just doing. Just doing* does not mean that one does not have a purpose, does not think, does not plan. But in imposing one's will and intentions on reality and on events, one does not lose the basic experience and joy of *just doing.* As a child retains the joy of *just seeing* as it learns to distinguish between the various things that it sees, so we must be able to *do* without losing the capacity to judge. Our problem is that we get wrapped up in what we are doing and why we are doing it — analyzing it, planning, worrying about it — so that we lose the joy that is always available — *of just doing.*

Just to be, just to do — these are the two great gifts of God, the foundations of every other gift. We need to return to these two great capacities again and again and cultivate them. The events of daily life need to be placed in perspective by a deep sense of prayer, by learning how to *be* before God. Then, as reality comes in upon us, we will perceive each event as the working of the Holy Spirit, carefully designed for our particular needs. Every event is a touch of the living finger of God, which is sketching in us — body, soul, and spirit — the true image of his Son, the being that the Father originally gave us and which he is restoring.

If we want to be anything other than what God has made us to be, we are wasting our time. It will not work. The greatest accomplishment in life is to be what we are, which is God's idea of what he wanted us to be when he brought us into being; and no ideas of ours will ever change it. Accepting that gift is accepting God's will for us, and in its acceptance lies the path to growth and ultimate fulfillment.

13

THE GRACE OF THE ASCENSION

By becoming a man Christ annihilated the dichotomy between matter and spirit. In the person of the God-man, a continuum between the divine and the human has been established. The incredible mystery of God's plan is not only to spiritualize the material universe, but to make matter itself *divine*. He has already done so in the glorified humanity of his Son. The grace bestowed on us by the ascension of Jesus is the divinization of *our* humanity. Our individuality is totally permeated by the Spirit of God through the grace of the ascension, and more specifically, through the grace of Pentecost. Thus, we too, in Christ, have annihilated the dichotomy between matter and spirit. Our life has become a mysterious interpenetration of material experience, spiritual reality, and the divine presence.

The key to being a Christian is to know Jesus Christ with the *whole* of our being. How great it is to know his sacred humanity through our senses and to reflect upon it with our reason, to treasure his teaching and example in our imagination and memory, and to imitate him by a life of moral integrity. But this

71

is only the beginning. It is to the transcendent potential in ourselves — to our mind which opens up to unlimited truth, and to our will which reaches out for unlimited love — that Christ addresses himself in the Gospel with particular urgency.

Not only is it essential to know Jesus Christ with the whole of our being; it is also essential to know Jesus Christ in the whole of *his* being. We must know Christ, first of all, in his sacred humanity and historical reality, and, more precisely, in his passion, which was the culminating point of his life on earth. The essential note of his passion is the emptying of his divinity. We enter into his emptying by accepting the emptying process in our own life, by laying aside our false self, and by living in the presence of God, the source of our being.

We must know Christ, however, not only in his human nature — in his passion and emptying, — but also in his divinity. This is the grace of the resurrection. It is the power to live his risen life. It is the grace *not* to sin. It is the grace to express his risen life in the face of our own inner poverty, but without ceasing to feel it.

The grace of the ascension offers a still more incredible union, a more entrancing invitation to unbounded life and truth. This is the invitation to enter into the Cosmic Christ — into his *divine* person, the Word of God, who has always been present in the world. And he has always been present in a saving way because of God's foreknowledge of his incarnation, death, and resurrection. Christ is "the light that enlightens everyone" (John 1:9) — the God who is secretly at work in the most unexpected, surprising, and hidden ways. This is the Christ who has disappeared in his ascension beyond the clouds, not into some geographical location, but *into the heart of all creation.* In particular, he has penetrated the very depths of our being, and our separateness has become submerged in his divine person, so that now we can act under the influence of his Spirit. Thus, even if we drink a cup of soup or walk down the street, it is Christ living and acting in us, transforming the world from within. This transformation appears in the guise of ordinary things — in the guise of our seemingly insignificant daily routine.

The ascension is Christ's return to the heart of all creation, where he dwells now in his glorified humanity. The mystery of his presence is hidden throughout creation and in every part of it. At some moment of history, which prophecy calls the Last Day, our eyes will be opened, and we will see reality as it is, which we know now only by faith. That faith reveals that Christ, dwelling at the center of all creation and of each individual member of it, is transforming it and bringing it back, in union with himself, into the bosom of the Father. Thus, the eternal glory of the Trinity is achieved through the maximum sharing of the divine life with every creature according to its capacity. This is the fulness of the divine plan, "the mystery hidden for ages in God" (Eph. 3:9).

The fruit of the grace of the ascension is the triumphant faith that believes that God's will is being done no matter what happens. It believes that creation is already glorified, though in a hidden manner, as it awaits the revelation of the sons of God.

The grace of the ascension enables us to perceive the irresistible power of the Spirit transforming everything into Christ, despite any and all appearances to the contrary. In the misery of the ghetto, the battlefield, the concentration camp; in the family torn by dissension; in the loneliness of the orphanage, old-age home, or hospital ward — wherever things seem to be disintegrating into grosser forms of matter and evil — the light of the ascension is burning with irresistible power. This is one of the greatest intuitions of faith. This faith finds Christ, not only in the beauty of nature, art, and human friendship, but also in the malice and injustice of men and in the inexplicable suffering of the innocent. Even there it finds the same infinite love expressing the hunger of God for us, a hunger that he intends to satisfy.

Thus, in Colossians, Paul does not hesitate to cry out with his triumphant faith in the ascension: "Christ *is* all, and in all" (Col. 3:11)—meaning *now*, not just in the future. At this moment we too have the grace to see Christ's light shining in our hearts; to feel his absorbing presence within us; and to perceive in every created thing—even in the most disconcerting—the presence of his love, his light, and his glory.

Pentecost also is both an event and a grace. So too are all the feasts of the Liturgical Year. The grace of Christmas is to know him in his humanity. The grace of Epiphany is to know him in his divinity. The grace of Holy Week is to know him in his emptying and dying. The grace of Easter is to know him in his triumph over sin and death. And the grace of the Ascension is to know him in the whole of his being, as the Cosmic Christ. It is to know the glorified Christ, who has passed, not into some geographical location, but into the depths of all creation.

The Cosmic Christ, revealed in the mystery of the Ascension, manifests our deep self and the inner nature of all reality. What is manifested is the living, vibrant Spirit, filling us and all things with boundless life and love. The Spirit is always present, yet always coming to us. That is because the divine actuality becomes present in a new way each time we move to a new level of spiritual awareness. The Spirit has been given; yet he is always waiting to be received so that he can give himself again—and more completely.

On the day of his resurrection, Jesus breathed his Spirit upon his disciples, saying: "Receive the Holy Spirit" (John 20:22). On the day of the ascension, forty days later, he "charged them not to depart from Jerusalem, but to wait for the promise of the Father . . . before many days, you shall be baptized with the Holy Spirit" (Acts 1:4-5).

The Spirit, then, is not given only once. He is an ongoing promise, an endless promise—a promise that is always fulfilled and always being fulfilled, because he is infinite and boundless and can never be fully plumbed.

The Spirit is the ultimate promise of the Father. A promise is a free gift. No one can be bound to make a promise. Once a promise is made, however, one is bound. When God binds himself, it is with absolute freedom, absolute fidelity. The Spirit, as a promise, is a gift, not a possession. He is a promise that has been communicated; hence, never to be taken back, since God is infinitely faithful to his promises. Note that the communication is by way of *gift*, not possession. Like the air we breathe, we can have all that we wish to take into our lungs; but it does not belong to us. If we try to take possession of it — stuff it in a closet for safekeeping — our efforts will be in vain. Air is not made to be possessed, and neither is the Spirit.

The divine Spirit functions in a similar way. He is all gift, but he will not acquiesce to a possessive attitude. He is all ours, as long as we give him away. "The wind blows where it wills and you hear the sound of it, but you do not know when it comes or whither it goes; so it is with everyone who is born of the Spirit" (John 3:8). In these words, Jesus explained to Nicodemus and to us that we have no control over him. In fact, it is in giving him away that we manifest that we truly have received him. He is the supreme gift, but supremely himself, supremely free.

The Spirit of God, *the* promise of the Father, sums up in himself all the promises of Christ. For they all point to him. The incarnation is a promise. The passion and death of Jesus are promises. His resurrection and ascension are each a promise. Pentecost itself, the outpouring of the Spirit, is a promise. All are promises and pledges of the divine Spirit, present and to be received at every moment. He is the last, the greatest, and the completion of all God's promises, the living summary of them all. Faith in him is faith in the whole of revelation. Openness and surrender to his guidance is the continuation of God's revelation in us and through us. It is to be involved in the redemption of the world, in the divinization of the whole universe. To know that Christ is all in all and to know his Spirit, the ongoing promise of the Father — this is the grace of Pentecost.

Between God and us, two extremes meet: He who is everything, and we who are nothing at all. It is the Spirit who makes us one with God and in God, just as the Word is with God and is God — the Word by nature; we by participation and communication. Our Lord prayed for this unity at the Last Supper. Many of his words on that occasion find their fulfillment and ultimate significance in the outpouring of the Spirit into our minds and hearts. Jesus said, "The glory you have given to me, I have given to them, that they may be one as we are one. I in them and you in me, that they may become perfectly one" (John 17:22-23).

Thus, we are not just *with* God in virtue of our baptism and our Christian vocation, we are *in* God. The Spirit is the gift of God, welling up in the Trinity from the common heart of the Father and the Son. He is the overflow of the divine life into the sacred humanity of Jesus, and then into the rest of us, his members.

When Jesus was talking to the Samaritan woman about the gift of God, he encouraged her to request it of him. He was sitting at the well as he spoke to her of the Spirit. The well is a symbol of what is deepest and most hidden, but which is our greatest potentiality — namely, our capacity to receive the Spirit, who communicates himself to us beyond thought and feeling in the substance of our spirit.

"If anyone thirst, let him come to me and drink. He who believes in me, as the scripture has said, 'Out of his heart will flow rivers of living water'" (John 7:37-38). John tells us that he was speaking of the Spirit when he said these words. The Spirit is the stream of living water which wells up in those who believe. It is the same Spirit that causes our hearts to rejoice because of the confidence that he inspires in God as Father. *Abba*, the word that spontaneously wells up in us, sums up our intimacy with God and our awareness of being not just *with* God, as friend to friend, but *in* God. We are penetrated by God and penetrating into God, through the mysterious, all-enveloping, all-absorbing, all-embracing Spirit.

Jesus in his priestly prayer for his disciples pleaded "that they may all be one; as you, Father, are in me, and I in you, that they also may be in us" (John 17:21). It is the Spirit who causes us to be one in the body of Christ. We have all received the same Spirit, enlivening us, causing us to be in Christ, in the Father, in the Spirit — to be *in* Christ, not just *with* him.

We are in God and he is in us, and the unifying force is the Spirit. To live in the Spirit is the fulfillment of every law and commandment, the sum of every duty to each other, and the joy of oneness with everything that is.

EPILOGUE

God has manifested himself, we Christians believe, in a new and extraordinary way in Jesus Christ; in a way which makes him more accessible to every human being through the super-abundance of grace which Jesus brought into the world. Once the art of thinking and feeling with Christ has developed through pondering the scriptures and has been deepened by contemplative prayer, we have to reflect on the signs of the times and what is to be done given the circumstances in which we find ourselves. We may be called to some special ministry, as Christ called his first disciples. Maybe we are called to reflect the Christian life in our own family and circle of friends, like the man out of whom the Lord cast a legion of demons. When he pressed to follow Jesus, he was told, "Go back home" — not to forget about his deliverance, but to share the new life he had received with his family and friends.

Whatever the circumstances, there is a Christian way of responding to them. Nowadays, when there are vast social problems which need Christian solutions, the signs of the times have to include not only our own immediate environment, but the broader world: the neighborhood, city, or nation, in which we live — indeed, the whole world and the future of the human race. Relying on the Holy Spirit, we must choose how to respond to the signs of the time out of our Christian tradition.

Tradition consists not only of handing down the dogmatic formulas and liturgical customs from one generation to the next. It means receiving this traditional teaching into ourselves in such a way that it becomes part of *us*. It must pass through our minds and hearts, become our own, and emerge in our lives as a true revelation of Christ here and now. It is only then that our baptism and the other sacraments achieve their purpose of extending Christ's presence throughout time and space. Christians are meant to be the continuing revelation of God's Son through the inspiration of his Holy Spirit who dwells within us. That inspiration can be more or less. It will be more in the degree that we penetrate the mystery of Christ to its depths. This can only be done through contemplative prayer and the abiding state of mystical union to which it leads. Then, under the influence of the gift of wisdom, we can grasp the meaning and significance of the truths of faith and express them with the kind of unction which comes from the Spirit.

The basic thrust of Christian spirituality might be summed up in two texts from the Old Testament which speak to the fundamental situation of the human adventure. The first is from Exodus: "I am who am" (Exod. 3:14). God thus reveals himself as unlimited being. *Is*-ness. Everything that *is* must be in relationship to his infinite being, and in fact, penetrated by it.

The other text is from Psalm 46:11: "Be still, and you shall know that I am God." We are thus invited to open ourselves completely to this infinite being, to the reality of the God who *is*; who penetrates, surrounds, and embraces us at every moment. God is the atmosphere that our spirit needs to breathe in order "to live, move, and have our being" (Acts 17:28).